A City Adventure in... London

by Amy Allatson

Words that look like *this* can be found in the glossary on page 24.

Contents

Page 4	What Is a City?
Page 6	Where Is London?
Page 8	Where and Why?
Page 10	Sightseeing in London
Page 12	Food in London
Page 14	Travelling around London
Page 16	Where Do People Live in London?
Page 18	Geography
Page 20	Out and About
Page 22	What Is it?
Page 23	Quick Quiz
Page 24	Glossary and Index

BookLife PUBLISHING

©This edition was published in 2023.
First published in 2018.

BookLife Publishing Ltd.
King's Lynn, Norfolk, PE30 4LS, UK

HB ISBN: 978-1-80155-919-5
PB ISBN: 978-1-80505-340-8

All rights reserved.
Printed in China.
A catalogue record for this book is available from the British Library.

Written by:
Amy Allatson

Edited by:
Charlie Ogden

Designed by:
Ian McMullen

MIX
Paper from responsible sources
FSC® C113515

All facts, statistics, web addresses and URLs in this book were verified as valid and accurate at time of writing. No responsibility for any changes to external websites or references can be accepted by either the author or publisher.

What Is a City?

Cities are **urban settlements**. They are bigger in size than towns and villages and have larger **populations**. Cities are usually very busy places with lots of buildings.

There are cities in every country, and most countries have a capital city. Cities are often home to people from many different **cultures**.

WHAT IS A CAPITAL CITY? A capital city is usually home to a country's government.

Where Is London?

London is the largest city in England. It is located in the south-east of England, around the River Thames.

Population: Over 9.5 million

Famous landmark: Big Ben

Language: English

Coldest months: December and January
Average temperature: 5 degrees Celsius

Warmest months: June and July
Average temperature: 18 degrees Celsius

B 83-64-49

London is the capital city of England. It is home to many people, including the **Prime Minister** and the British Royal Family.

Where and Why?

A group of people called the Romans settled in the city of London nearly 2,000 years ago. The Romans chose the land because it was close to the River Thames.

The Romans called London 'Londinium'.

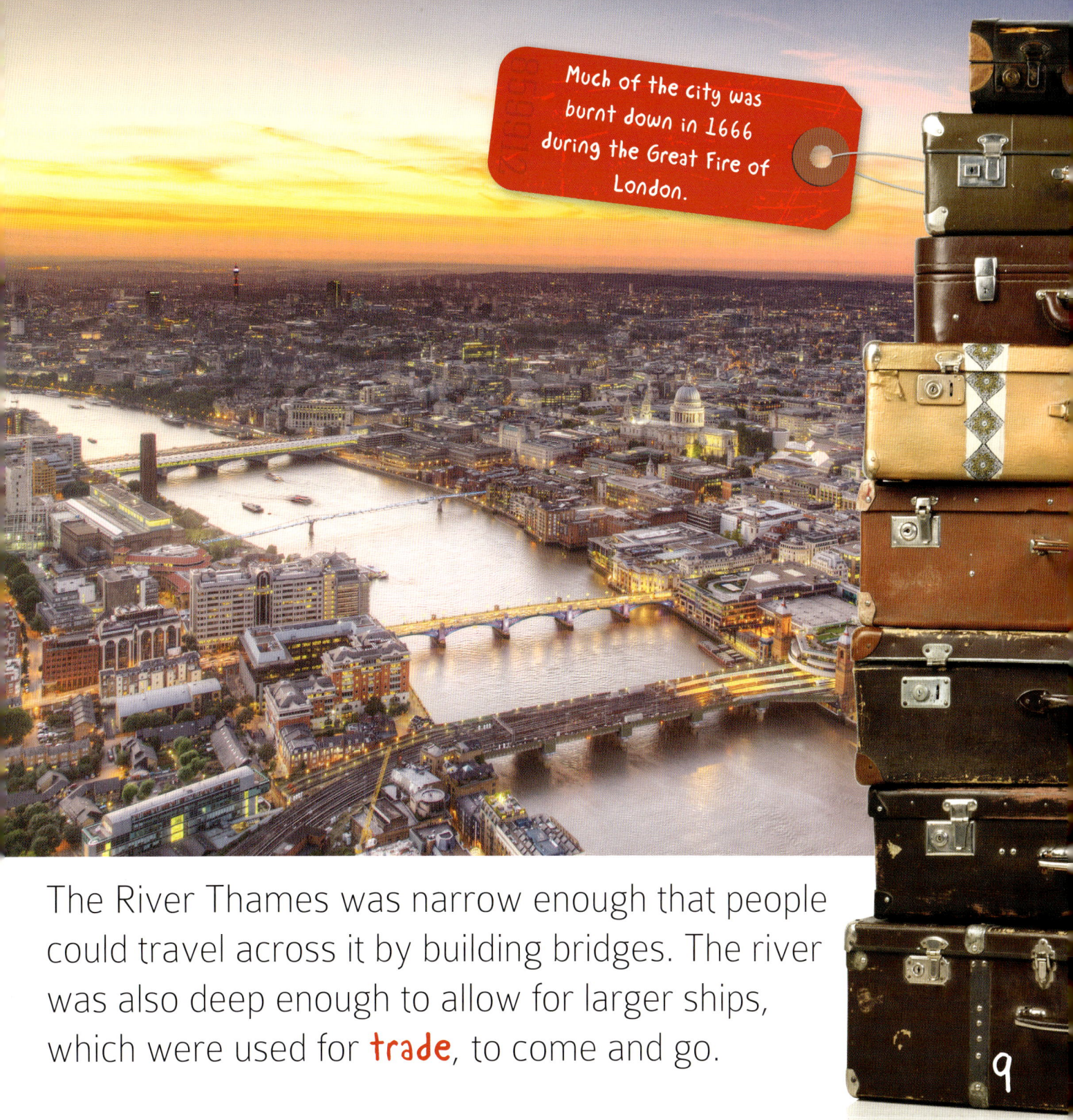

Much of the city was burnt down in 1666 during the Great Fire of London.

The River Thames was narrow enough that people could travel across it by building bridges. The river was also deep enough to allow for larger ships, which were used for **trade**, to come and go.

Sightseeing in London

This is the Elizabeth Tower at the Palace of Westminster. The nickname for the bell inside the tower is 'Big Ben'.

There are many things to see and do in London. **Tourists** can visit the Houses of Parliament and Big Ben at the Palace of Westminster. This is where members of the government work.

Tourists can visit the West End to see a musical or a play. Tourists can also visit Buckingham Palace to see the Royal Family's home.

Buckingham Palace

The Queen's Guard keep Buckingham Palace safe.

Food in London

London has many restaurants and street markets where people can buy food. These places sell lots of different types of food from all around the world.

Pie and mash

Pie and mash is a **traditional** meal that first appeared in London. The pie is usually filled with meat or vegetables and is served with mashed potatoes. People often eat the dish with mushy peas and gravy.

Travelling around London

Some people travel around London on an underground **railway network** called the London Underground. The trains travel underneath the city at high speeds.

In London, the Underground is often called the 'Tube'.

Some people in London travel by bus.

A traditional London bus is usually bright red with two floors. It is called a double-decker bus.

Where Do People Live in London?

Lots of people who live in London live in *modern* flats in very tall buildings.

Number 10 Downing Street is over 300 years old and contains over 90 rooms.

London is home to many famous people. The Prime Minister of the UK lives at 10 Downing Street.

17

Geography

The River Thames is one of the longest rivers in England.

The River Thames flows through the middle of London. There are several famous bridges on the river, such as Westminster Bridge and Tower Bridge.

Westminster Bridge

Tower Bridge is a special type of bridge that can open up in the middle to let large boats through.

Open

Closed

Out and About

Hyde Park is London's biggest park. People can do lots of activities here, such as going boating on the lake and riding horses.

In the summer months, you can even go swimming in the park.

Tourists often see the city and its sights by travelling on a river boat or a double-decker bus.

River boat

What Is It?

Can you write down what's in the pictures below?

These are all things that are found in London.

Quick Quiz

1. How many people live in London?

2. Can you name a famous landmark in London?

3. What river is London built around?

4. What can you eat in London?

5. Who lives at 10 Downing Street?

Glossary

cultures	attitudes and beliefs of a country or a group of people
degrees Celsius	a way of saying how hot or cold something is
government	a group of people who make a country's rules and laws
modern	something from recent or present times
populations	the number of people who live in certain places
Prime Minister	the leader of a country's government
railway network	connected railway tracks and stations
tourists	people who are away from home because they are on holiday
trade	to buy and sell goods
traditional	something that has continued in a culture for a long time without changing
urban settlements	places where lots of people live and work, like towns or cities

Index

Big Ben 6, 10
bridges 9, 18–19
Buckingham Palace 11
buildings 4, 9, 16

food 12
Hyde Park 20
Prime Minister 7, 17
River Thames 6, 8–9, 18

Romans, the 8
tourists 10–11, 21
travelling 9, 14–15, 21

Photo Credits

Front Cover – 1, 5 – Zarya Maxim Alexandrovich. 2 – pisaphotography. 4 – CroMary. 6 – PHOTOCREO Michal Bednarek. 7 – Alex Yeung. 8 – Iakov Kalinin. 9 – Skoda, SVnova. 10 – Bikeworldtravel. 11 – Tulchinskaya, Leonid Andronov. 12 – Brian S. 13 – Monkey Business Images. 14 – JuliusKielaitis, Lucian Milasan0. 15 – James Steidl. 16 – yampi. 17 – pcruciatti, Daniel Gale. 18–19 – S.Borisov, Andrew Barker. 20 – MJSquared Photography. 21 – Samot.
All images are courtesy of Shutterstock.com, unless otherwise specified. With thanks to Getty Images, Thinkstock Photo and iStockphoto.